The Mouse in the Manor House

and other poems

Written by Sam Garland
Illustrated by Dan Long

To the Reddit community:

I owe, it's true, an ode or two
To all of those above:
This book, my friends, is made for you -
With deepest thanks and love.

Sprog.

PROLOGUE

TIME – with which we start and end –
Is rather strange indeed.
We've really quite a lot, my friend,
And never all we need.

I'm sure you've often heard it said:
'The time just passed me by' –
For time can ebb, or race ahead,
Or flit, or drag, or fly.

You've heard it said before, I'm sure,
That moments pass like days –
Or weeks like months, and months as more –
In many different ways.

And yet, despite the awful fuss,
In truth, our moments crawl –
And if they're *still* too fast for us,
Then what of creatures small?

In all the time (if one compares)
A child might learn to play,
A *mouse* is born, and grows, and pairs,
And dies with whiskers grey.

And so it stands to reason, friend,
These days that move at speed –
Or pass too quick, and quickly end –
For mice, are long indeed.

So join me in the Manor House,
And listen when I say –
'Twas Christmas Eve, and Peter Mouse,
Was missing for a day. . .

I.

We start with scenes of Christmas bliss
(For tone, you understand) –
The snow had laid a winter's kiss
Across a frozen land.

The gifts were wrapped; the children slept.
They dreamt of Santa's sleigh.
The house was set and cleaned and swept...
While minutes slipped away.

A pocket-watch The Big had dropped
(Though always loud and slow)
Had ticked and tocked its last and stopped
An hour or more ago.

And so poor Jenny Mouse, bereft,
Had not a way to see
How long it was since Peter left,
And where that mouse could be.

She paced and sighed, with whiskers pale.
She waited by the door.
She checked the clock (to no avail)
For half the night, or more.

(In truth, she felt those moments fast
And couldn't hope to know
The length of time that really passed –
Her estimates were low.)

He'd only gone to get some cheese –
A moment's work at most!
'A slice,' she'd said, 'or maybe, please,
A crumb or two of toast.'

But that was *oh-so-long-ago*,
And Christmas day was near –
Her pups would wake, and soon, and know
Their father wasn't here!

Perhaps he'd gotten trapped a while!
She thought with swift distress.

The house was safe.
She forced a smile.

The house was safe.

Unless...

*

2.

When Peter Mouse had left the Hole,
The Big had gone to bed.
He'd grabbed his bag and wooden bowl
For salt and cheese and bread.

He left with Christmas thoughts in mind
Of gifts and trees and snow.
He left his Jenny safe behind
(And Max and Eve and Flo).

He'd crept beneath the larder door
Without a second's glance -
He'd done it *lots* of times before...

And never had a chance.

*

3.

The hall was still and cold as ice,
For while The Big would sleep –
No fire was lit, with which the mice
Might steal a piece to keep.

She hurried by the frozen coal,
And passed the empty grate –
She climbed and crossed a curtain pole,
And faced the kitchen straight.

Her heart was quick; it beat and caught,
As horrors crossed her mind.
The door that lay in front, she thought,
Could hold her *death* behind.

For while she sat at home to wait
For Peter to return,
An awful thought had gathered weight,
And then begun to *burn*.

*

4.

When Jenny mouse was but a pup
(Twelve months ago, at that),
Her Uncle Fred was eaten up
And swallowed by a cat.

Oh, commonplace! I hear you say –
A cat that ate a mouse?
That happens almost every day!

... But not in Manor House.

The Big had shooed the thin and fat
Alike, her grandpa said –
So not a mouse had died of cat...
Until her Uncle Fred.

He'd gone for Christmas cheese, you know,
And captured in the act.
Her Uncle Fred, a year ago.

A year ago... exact.

*

5.

A tiny candle burned beside
The kitchen table, small –
It flit and tripped, then sent a tide
Of shadows up the wall.

She wriggled in and looked around,
But everything was still.
No cat (or Peter) to be found,
But shade and winter's chill.

And so it was on Christmas Eve,
Apart forevermore,
She wiped at tears, then turned to leave. . .
And spied the larder door.

(*'Of course he's there!'* I hear you moan.
'He went for cheese, you said!'
But Jenny Mouse was all alone,
And fear had filled her head.)

She crept toward it, keeping low,
And frightened to the fur –
Then heard a sound – a rumble, slow;
An awful, gruesome... *purr.*

It's hard to say what Jenny thought
To hear that frightful sound –
The dreadful waking dreams it brought
To crowd and gather round.

And yet, she never thought to flee,
Nor run, or quit her quest –
So think a while on bravery
While I relate the rest.

*

6.

He splashed and cried aloud and fought
For breath with every scream –
Her husband, Peter, trapped and caught
And drowned in bowls of cream!

He tried to swim the swollen tides
As vision turned to black –
But every time he reached the sides
The cat would push him back!

And there it was – a monstrous thing
Of sharpened tooth and claw;
In horror, Jenny heard it sing
Beneath the larder door:

'Will I watch as water wheeling,
Rolling up and rumbling, reeling,
Sinks this slip-shod ship's mouse, stealing
Breath away with glee?'

'Will these winter-winds, I wonder,
Split his sodden sails asunder,
Fighting through the foam and thunder,
Under such a sea?

'Will this mouse in milky-motion,
Make it through my nasty notion –
Cooked inside a creamy ocean
All for mighty me?'

At that, the cat produced a grin,
And laughed with vile delight –
While Jenny, frightened, listened in,
And shivered in the night.

Her heart was beating, *rat-a-tat*,
But what could Jenny do?
She couldn't hope to fight a cat,
And *that*, poor Jenny knew!

She spun around with nimble grace,
To search for some escape –
The candlewick. . . the fireplace. . .

A plan began to shape.

*

7

Its eyes were old and cold as night –
They glittered grim with death.
They watched the mouse with dark delight,
While Peter fought for breath.

He splished and splashed and sploshed and spun,
And tossed and turned about –
And when his race was almost run. . .
The feline fished him out!

'Mice,' it sighed, with false regret,
'Are such a tragic bore.
We've barely played a moment yet –
I'd rather hoped for more.'

It aired a sigh, and shook its head,
Then twitched its tail and frowned –
'So any final words?' it said,
And flicked the mouse around.

The mouse, afraid, and soaking wet,
And icy-frozen-cold,
Arose before the putrid pet,
And answered, brave and bold:

'You hateful, horrid, awful beast!
It's Christmas Eve!' he cried.
'So do it kind and quick, at least,
You *brute!'* said Pete, with pride.

The cat prepared its teeth to chew.
It licked its lips and grinned...
But staggered back as swiftly blew
A sudden gust of wind!

It wheezed behind the door and then,
As cold and dry as death,
It parried back and came again,
Like something's ghastly breath!

'Who's there?' exclaimed the cat in fear,
And raised a readied paw –
A light began to glow and near
Behind the larder door...

'Who's there?' exclaimed the cat, agape,
As shadows climbed the wall.
They gathered 'round and formed a shape;
A mouse – but six foot tall!

'RELEASE THE MOUSE!' the shade cried out,
And turned its mighty head:
The cat recoiled in fear and doubt,
And, cringing, slowly said:

'It's mine! I found it, fair and square!
I'll trade you, mouse for cheese!'
There came another blast of air,
And stormy, breathing wheeze.

'RELEASE THE MOUSE!' the shape replied,
And cried a warning-wail:
'FOR IF YOU DON'T, I'LL COME INSIDE
AND *EAT YOU*, NOSE TO TAIL!'

The cat was stunned and unprepared!
It scrambled 'cross the floor –
Then bounded through the window, scared,
And troubled mice no more.

The shadow waved a hand goodbye,
And jumped for joy, surprised –
It laughed a laugh, and sighed a sigh,
That Peter recognised!

He ran towards the larder door,
And in to Manor House –
He ran with hope and glee and more,
And there... was Jenny Mouse.

*

8.

Of course, by now I'm sure you know
Precisely what occurred –
The shadow-shape; the golden-glow;
The breath they felt and heard;

But if, perhaps, your thoughts are dazed,
I'll tell you now because –
You really ought to be amazed
How clever Jenny was!

To see her husband sunk in cream,
And captured by the cat –
The little mouse had planned a scheme
In twenty seconds flat!

She'd rushed across the kitchen floor,
And fetched the candle, lit –
She dragged it near the larder door,
And watched it flick and flit.

And then, with haste and loath to wait,
She grabbed her second part –
The bellows by the fire grate –
And made her fearless start.

The bellows blew! The candle glowed!
And though the mouse was small –
Her shadow, huge and giant, showed
Upon the larder wall!

… And this was all that Jenny said,
While Peter, speechless, sighed.
He kissed her hands and arms and head:
'*You clever mouse!*' he cried.

'But wait,' he said, 'now what about
The *voice* when I was trapped?'
She took a breath, and shouted out:

'LIKE THIS!'

And Peter clapped.

*

9.

The snow was falling, fine and white,
And there in Manor House,
There slept beneath the candle-light
A tiny little mouse.

Her husband, Peter, lay beside,
With little snuffles slow –
Her children dreamed of presents tied,
And footsteps in the snow.

We'll leave them here, with Peter freed,
And end this Christmas rhyme –
Their story's told.

They've all they need.

For now, and all of time.

*

Other Poems

Living Free

To float
and flit
and flap
and fly
Across a starlit
starry sky,
Would surely
really
rather be
A lovely thing,
It seems
to me.

To slip
and sail
and swoop
and soar
Through rainbow-rain
And clouds and more,
Would surely
really
rather be
A tiny taste
of living
free.

Come With Me

I have dreamt of a space in a faraway place
Under little-leaf leaves with the loon,
Where the wiffle-winds blow and the kitty-cats grow
In the shade of a silvery moon.

I have sung for their songs and I've bongoed the bongs
By the fire in time with the beat.
What a hoot! What a wiz! What a feeling it is
From your brow to the toes on your feet!

I have spied them at night by the loveliest light
From the stars of a singular sky.
Come on by, follow me –
Oh what wonders we'll see!
Oh how happy we'll be, you and I!

Her Ladyship's Ploy

Came the sound of a call through the Manor House hall
From the dignified Lady Marie:
"There's a hideous mouse in my beautiful house!
Oh won't somebody smush it for me?"

So the dukes and the lords with their decorative swords
All arose to the challenge with joy –
And they ran and they raced and they rumbled and chased,
Unaware of her Ladyship's ploy.

(For the Lady Marie had a problem, you see,
And she needed a husband to wed.
All her wealth had its fate in her marital state,
And the occupancy of her bed.

She imagined a plan to acquire a man,
And she thought of a marvellous test –
For the person that caught that creation, she thought,
Would of course be the brightest and best!)

But in moments she knew that her plan wouldn't do,
As she watched, disappointed with doubt –
For they spun and they stabbed and they groped and they grabbed
Till her hall was in tatters thoughout.

"Oh good heavens!" she said, with a shake of her head,
"Well that rodent's the brains of the house!"
So she bid them good day, and she sent them away...
And she married the manor-hall mouse.

When There's a Wind...

When there's a wind that blows and sighs,
And clouds that seem to stay
Forever looming in the sky
To quell the brightest day;

I close the door against the rain,
Against the dark and more –
And wait for it to pass again,
Just like it did before.

Whilst walking to the city...

Whilst walking to the city
On my way to buy a hat,
I met an itty-bitty
Little city kitty-cat.

Its ears were short and scabby
And its coat was rough to boot –
But when I moved that shabby
Flabby tabby followed suit!

'Well goodness me and golly!'
So I spoke and stroked its fur.
'I ought to call you Molly,
Jolly puss, or Polly-purr!

I'm off to fetch some leather
For a cap when skies are dull;
But we could stay together
Whether weather's fair or full!

So come on, little kitty,
To the city – you and me!
You're oh-so-itty-bitty,
Oh, what pretty sights we'll see!'

My Undead Uncle

When Uncle Stanley breathed his last
And finally bit the dust,
He never knew his time had passed
And thought the act unjust.

The priest had spoke a sad 'amen'
And blessed my dad and me –
When Stanley got back up again,
And came 'round ours for tea.

I'll tell you this: though ghost or ghoul
(And most a monstrous man),
There's really no one quite as cool
As undead Uncle Stan!

A Vagrant Unveiled

There was a man
Whose clothes were rags,
All tied with string
And paper-bags.

Though others laughed,
And pointed too,
He knew
precisely
what to do.

He didn't cry.
He didn't bawl.

He simply wore no clothes at all.

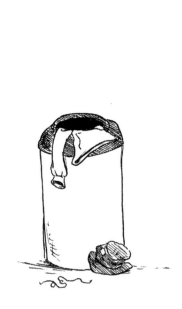

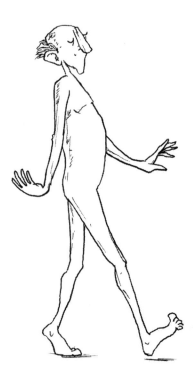

Ratatat

When Ratatat,
The giant cat,
Came round one night for tea,
I tried and tried
To match his stride,
But he ate more than me.

Size doesn't matter

Despite I'll never understand
The universe's size,
Or that I'm baffled by the distance
Of the stars in skies;
And even though, if I could walk
The space between the black,
I'd find myself alone and lost
And never make it back;
I've always felt, and always will,
That though, to some degree,
I may be insignificant...
There's only one of me.

Made in the USA
Lexington, KY
07 July 2017

The Mouse in the Manor House (and other poems) is
the first published collection of poetry by Sam Garland.
Sam lives in the UK and has made a hobby of posting origi-
nal poetry on the website "reddit.com" under the username
"Poem_for_your_sprog."

'**Sprog**': British - *informal humorous*. A child.

'**Poem_for_your_sprog**': British - *occasionally humorous*.
1. Rhymes in the style of children's poetry.
2. Literally – *a poem for your sprog.*

ISBN 9781512307481

9 781512 307481

Jennifer Eloff

Les desserts sans sucre

LOW-CALORIE SWEETENER

Recettes à base
de granulé SPLENDA®

LES ÉDITIONS DE
L'HOMME